Western Europe, A.D. 804

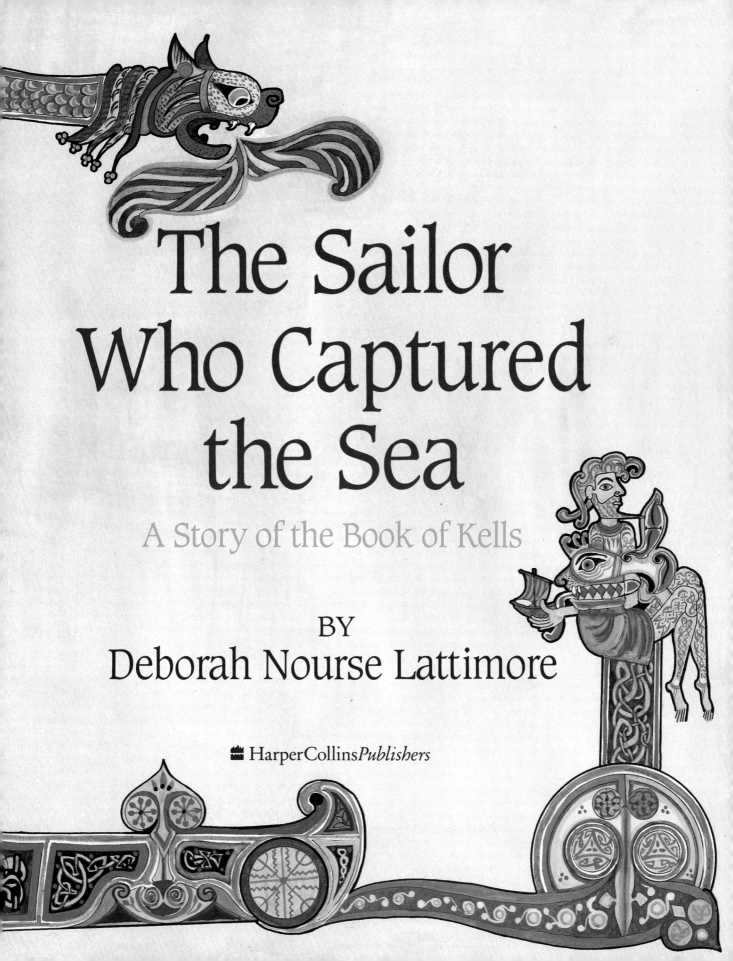

The Sailor Who Captured the Sea

A Story of the Book of Kells

BY
Deborah Nourse Lattimore

HarperCollins*Publishers*

To my husband, Steve,
and our children, Nicholas, Isabel, and Judith,
and to all my creative friends, who persevere

The Sailor Who Captured the Sea: A Story of the Book of Kells
Copyright © 1991 by Deborah Nourse Lattimore
Printed in the U.S.A. All rights reserved.
Typography by Andrew J. Rhodes
2   3   4   5   6   7   8   9   10

Library of Congress Cataloging-in-Publication Data
Lattimore, Deborah Nourse.
    The sailor who captured the sea : a story of the Book of Kells /
by Deborah Nourse Lattimore.
        p.   cm.
    Summary: A sailor continues the work of others in creating the
illuminated Book of Kells.
    ISBN 0-06-023710-4.—ISBN 0-06-023711-2 (lib. bdg.)
    1. Bible. N.T. Gospels. Latin. Book of Kells—Juvenile literature.
[1. Bible. N.T. Gospels. Latin. Book of Kells.   2. Illumination of books
and manuscripts.]   I. Title.
ND3359.K4L38   1991   89-26937
745.6′7′0941822—dc20   CIP
                                                              AC

The illustrations for THE SAILOR WHO CAPTURED THE SEA were executed
on ninety-pound hot press D'Arches watercolor paper with Winsor
& Newton tube watercolor. They were pretreated with a light wash
to simulate a parchment look.

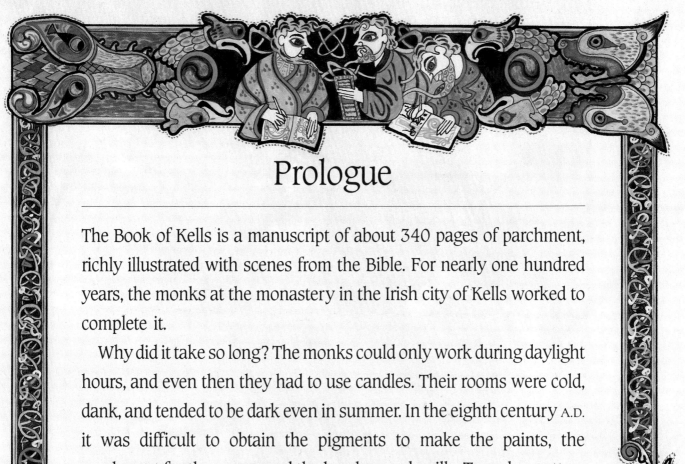

Prologue

The Book of Kells is a manuscript of about 340 pages of parchment, richly illustrated with scenes from the Bible. For nearly one hundred years, the monks at the monastery in the Irish city of Kells worked to complete it.

Why did it take so long? The monks could only work during daylight hours, and even then they had to use candles. Their rooms were cold, dank, and tended to be dark even in summer. In the eighth century A.D. it was difficult to obtain the pigments to make the paints, the parchment for the pages, and the brushes and quills. To make matters worse, the monks were constantly threatened by invasions from the Vikings and by assaults from neighboring Irish kings. The monks hid the book during invasions and brought it out to work on again when all was safe.

With admirable single-mindedness the monks seem to have been driven to finish the book. Almost everyone worked on it; some were especially good at lettering, and others specialized in geometric patterns, animals, or people. Since they were most skilled at making interlaced designs, they filled the book with magnificently ornate, intricate patterns unlike anything ever seen in that part of the world.

Why was it so important to make just one fine book? What drove them to pursue their goal in the face of such great difficulties? Perhaps only the beautiful Book of Kells—now on display at Trinity College in Dublin—can provide the answer.

IN the year of the Lord 804, near the Port of Dubh-linn, there lived three brothers. Fursa, the oldest, was a strong-armed boy with a generous nature who, when he grew up, became a stonecutter. Niall, the middle brother, was a serious, quiet lad who grew up to be a metalsmith. Broghan, the youngest, went from one thing to another until he became, at last, a sailor and was happy.

One day news came that Viking ships had attacked several northern ports of Ireland. Many people fled inland to the town of Kells and the monastery of St. Columba. Fursa and Niall gathered up their few belongings.

"We are going to the monastery," said Fursa. "Come with us."

"That is fine for you and Niall," replied Broghan. "But I cannot leave the sea."

Broghan bade them farewell. But as the months passed, fewer captains braved the sea for fear of attacks by Viking ships. Broghan found less and less work. He missed his brothers. At last, he too set out for Kells.

After three days' walking Broghan reached the watch-tower of the great monastery. Fursa himself met Broghan with an embrace and led him to the scriptorium, where holy books were copied. There Niall greeted Broghan warmly.

"We gave up our trades," he explained, "and worked hard to become artists. Finishing the Great Book of Gospels is our most important task."

"According to an ancient law," Fursa went on, "once the Book is completed, no one, not an Irish king nor a Viking lord, can attack us again."

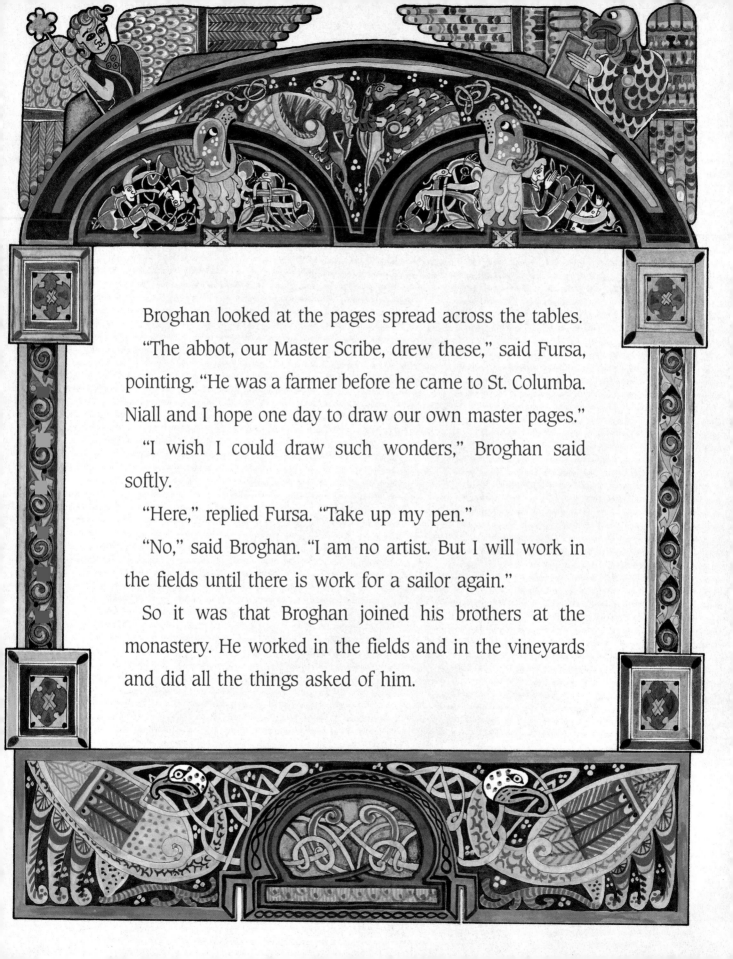

Broghan looked at the pages spread across the tables.

"The abbot, our Master Scribe, drew these," said Fursa, pointing. "He was a farmer before he came to St. Columba. Niall and I hope one day to draw our own master pages."

"I wish I could draw such wonders," Broghan said softly.

"Here," replied Fursa. "Take up my pen."

"No," said Broghan. "I am no artist. But I will work in the fields until there is work for a sailor again."

So it was that Broghan joined his brothers at the monastery. He worked in the fields and in the vineyards and did all the things asked of him.

Soon the old abbot wished to return to his homeland on the island of Iona. Broghan took him by oxcart to the coast and helped him board his ship.

"How I love the feel of a boat!" Broghan thought, breathing the salt air. He picked up a small conch shell, held it to his ear, and listened to its ocean murmur. And though the breeze tugged at his sleeves, Broghan slowly turned back toward Kells, the shell nestled in his cloak.

With the abbot now gone, Fursa became the Master Scribe.

"Come, Broghan," said Fursa. "It is time you practiced with your pen. We must finish the Book of Gospels quickly and will need everyone's help."

"I am a sailor, not a scribe," Broghan said, shaking his head.

"Help us," said Niall. "You will find, as did I, that your hand grows surer with practice."

But try as he might, Broghan could not draw as well as his brothers. One day he slipped away and walked toward the sea. In the lowland mists he listened vainly for the calls of seabirds and imagined the sea brimming with ships. "Soon I'll be on a ship again, where I belong," Broghan said to himself, and he held the conch shell to his ear.

The next day word came that the old abbot had died in his sleep on Iona. Fursa put down his pen, took up his chisel, and carved a stone cross in the abbot's memory. Weeks later, when it was completed, the monks raised it on its foundation. Suddenly a shout came from the watchtower. The king of Tara appeared at the gate.

"War is expensive," he told the monks. "My men need gold for their purses and meat to fill their stomachs." He motioned to his soldiers, who rushed to the fields to herd the cattle.

"Wait!" said Fursa. "The animals you may take. But whatever treasure we have belongs to God and this monastery."

Then the king spied the great stone cross.

"Let the man who carved this cross come to my castle to be my stonecutter. In exchange I will allow your monastery to stand."

Fursa knew that many other monasteries had been burned to the ground by invading kings. He embraced his brothers and left.

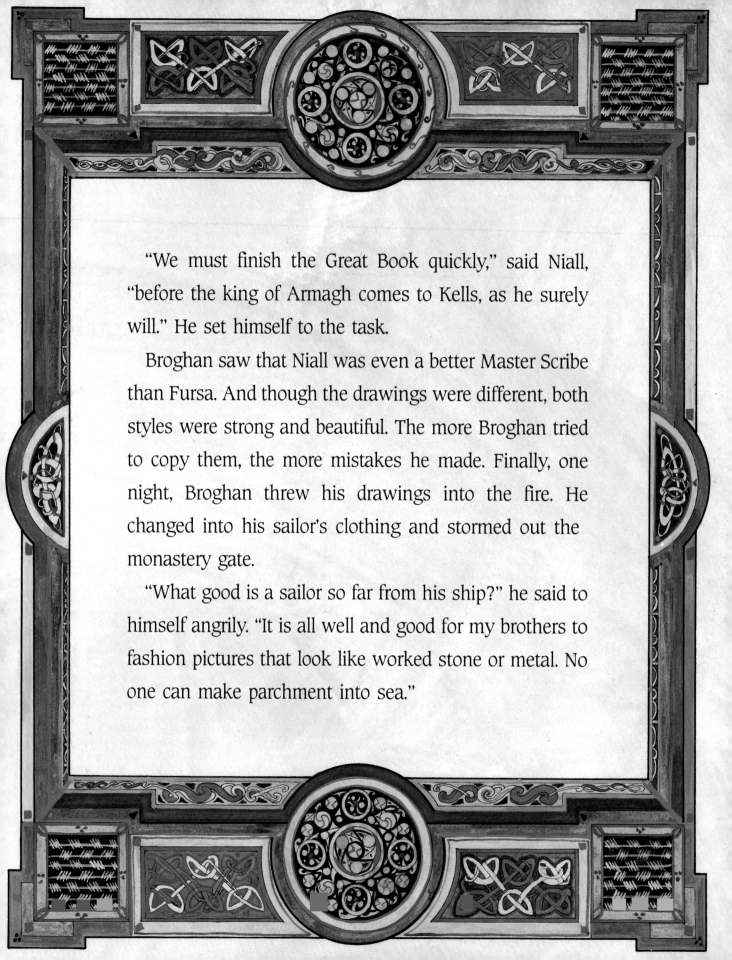

"We must finish the Great Book quickly," said Niall, "before the king of Armagh comes to Kells, as he surely will." He set himself to the task.

Broghan saw that Niall was even a better Master Scribe than Fursa. And though the drawings were different, both styles were strong and beautiful. The more Broghan tried to copy them, the more mistakes he made. Finally, one night, Broghan threw his drawings into the fire. He changed into his sailor's clothing and stormed out the monastery gate.

"What good is a sailor so far from his ship?" he said to himself angrily. "It is all well and good for my brothers to fashion pictures that look like worked stone or metal. No one can make parchment into sea."

When Broghan felt the cool sand beneath his feet, he scanned the horizon for a ship.

"A Viking boat," yelled a villager running up the shore.

Broghan saw a small, battered boat, its mainmast cracked, pitch violently over the waves. A young boy clung

to the lines. Without hesitation Broghan flung himself into the crashing surf. He swam to the boat and climbed on. He tied up the mast and guided the boat to shore.

Broghan saw that the boy was not hurt. He covered him with his cloak and built a good fire.

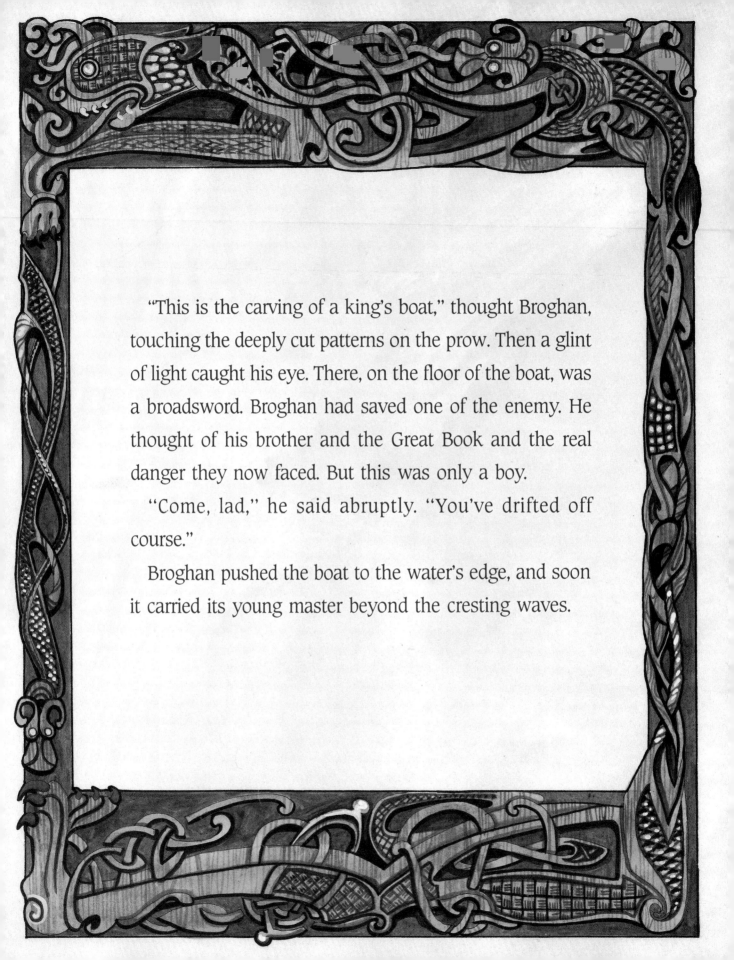

"This is the carving of a king's boat," thought Broghan, touching the deeply cut patterns on the prow. Then a glint of light caught his eye. There, on the floor of the boat, was a broadsword. Broghan had saved one of the enemy. He thought of his brother and the Great Book and the real danger they now faced. But this was only a boy.

"Come, lad," he said abruptly. "You've drifted off course."

Broghan pushed the boat to the water's edge, and soon it carried its young master beyond the cresting waves.

Broghan hastened back to Kells to warn Niall and the others. But it was Brother Donnan who descended the watchtower to meet him.

"Thank God you have returned," said Brother Donnan. "The king of Armagh came, and Niall went with him to do service as his metalsmith. What shall we do?"

"You will keep a good watch for Vikings," said Broghan. "And I will try to finish the Great Book."

Broghan picked up his pen and began to draw. This time, instead of trying to draw like Fursa or Niall, he thought of the sea. Slowly and awkwardly at first, then more easily, with a thin, light line, he soon completed page after page.

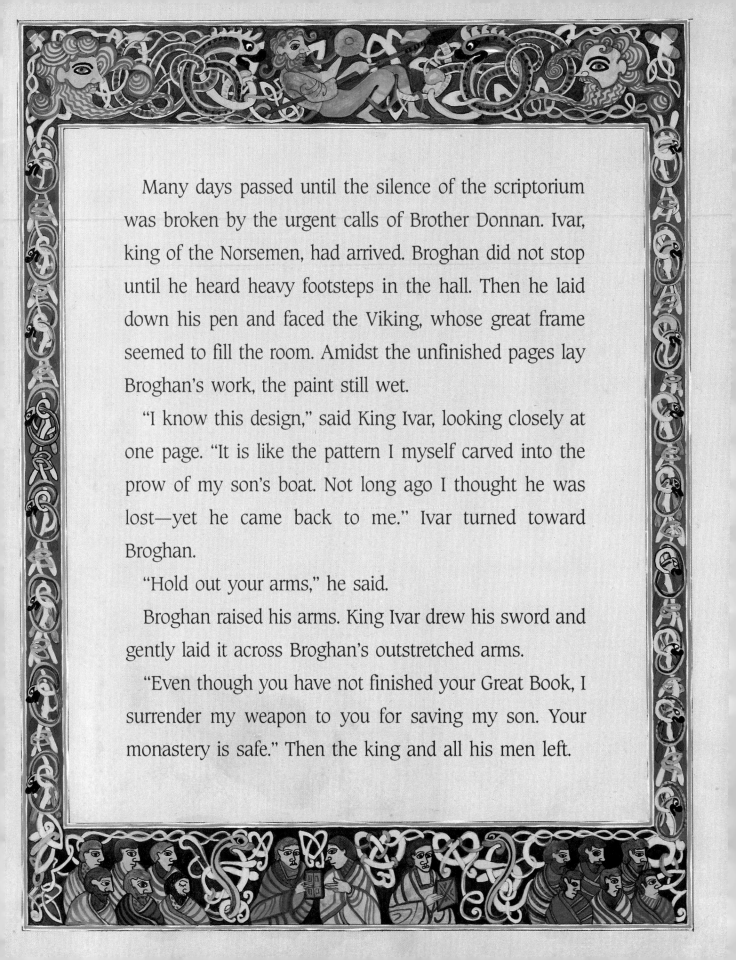

Many days passed until the silence of the scriptorium was broken by the urgent calls of Brother Donnan. Ivar, king of the Norsemen, had arrived. Broghan did not stop until he heard heavy footsteps in the hall. Then he laid down his pen and faced the Viking, whose great frame seemed to fill the room. Amidst the unfinished pages lay Broghan's work, the paint still wet.

"I know this design," said King Ivar, looking closely at one page. "It is like the pattern I myself carved into the prow of my son's boat. Not long ago I thought he was lost—yet he came back to me." Ivar turned toward Broghan.

"Hold out your arms," he said.

Broghan raised his arms. King Ivar drew his sword and gently laid it across Broghan's outstretched arms.

"Even though you have not finished your Great Book, I surrender my weapon to you for saving my son. Your monastery is safe." Then the king and all his men left.

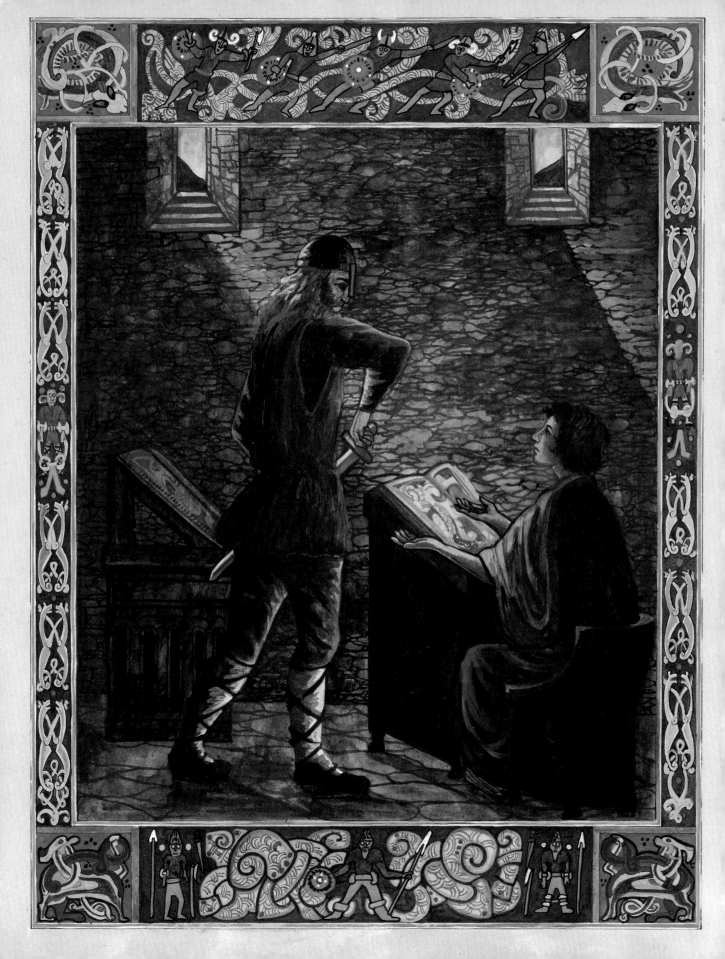

Of the three brothers from Dubh-linn, Broghan alone
remained at the monastery and finished the Great Book.
He had only to look at his brothers' drawings to feel their
presence clearly.

And never again did he miss the sea.

Ireland, A.D. 804